GOD GLORIFIED IN MAN'S DEPENDENCE

GOD

GLORIFIED

IN MAN'S

DEPENDENCE

Preached on the publick lecture in Boston, July 8, 1731; and published
at the desire of several ministers and others, in Boston, who heard it.

JONATHAN EDWARDS, A.M.

Pastor of the Church of CHRIST in *Northampton*.

---

*Lest Israel vaunt themselves against me, saying, mine own hand
hath saved me.*—JUDGES 7:2.

CURIOSMITH

MINNEAPOLIS

Published by Curiosmith.
P. O. Box 390293, Minneapolis, Minnesota, 55439.
Internet: curiosmith.com.
E-mail: shopkeeper@curiosmith.com.

Previously—Boston: Printed by S. Kneeland, and T. Green, for D. Henchman, at the Corner Shop on the South-side of the Town-House. 1731.

The text of this edition is from *Works of Jonathan Edwards,* edited by Edward Hickman, 1843.

Scripture verse footnotes are from *The Holy Bible*, King James Version, and have been added to this edition.

The "Outline of the Contents" was added to this edition by the publisher.

Note: Acts 2:13 changed to Acts 2:38. (Page 28.)

Supplementary content and cover design:

ISBN 9781935626800

OUTLINE OF THE CONTENTS
————∘∘⦂⦂∘∘————

(Outline of the Contents is continued on the next page.)

ADVERTISEMENT TO THE READER

IT was with no small difficulty that the author's youth and modesty were prevailed on to let him appear a preacher in our public lecture, and afterwards to give us a copy of his discourse, at the desire of divers ministers and others who heard it. But as we quickly found him a workman that needs not to be ashamed before his brethren, our satisfaction was the greater to see him pitching upon so noble a subject, and treating it with so much strength and clearness, as the judicious reader will perceive in the following composure: a subject which secures to God his great design in the work of fallen man's redemption by the Lord Jesus Christ, which is evidently so laid out, as that the glory of the whole should return to him, the blessed ordainer, purchaser, and applier; a subject which enters deep into practical religion; without the belief of which, that must soon die in the hearts and lives of men.

For in proportion to the sense we have of our

dependence on the sovereign God for all the good we want, will be our value for him, our application to him, our trust in him, our fear to offend him, and our care to please him; as likewise our gratitude and love, our delight and praise, upon our sensible experience of his free benefits.

In short, it is the very soul of piety, to apprehend and own that all our springs are in him; the springs of our present grace and comfort, and of our future glory and blessedness; and that they all entirely flow through Christ, by the efficacious influence of the Holy Spirit. By these things saints live, and in all these things is the life of our spirits.

Such doctrines as these, which, by humbling the minds of men, prepare them for the exaltations of God, he has signally owned and prospered in the reformed world, and in our land especially, in the days of our forefathers; and we hope they will never grow unfashionable among us: for, we are well assured, if those which we call the doctrines of grace ever come to be contemned or disrelished, vital piety will proportionably languish and wear away; as these doctrines always sink in the esteem of men upon the decay of serious religion.

We cannot therefore but express our joy and thankfulness, that the great Head of the church is pleased still to raise up from among the children of his people, for the supply of his churches, those who assert and maintain these evangelical principles; and that our churches (notwithstanding all their degeneracies) have still a high value for such principles, and for those who publicly own and teach them.

And as we cannot but wish and pray that the college in the neighbouring colony (as well as our own) may be a fruitful mother of many such sons as the author, by the blessing of Heaven on the care of their present worthy rector; so we heartily rejoice in the special favour of Providence in bestowing such a rich gift on the happy church of Northampton, which has for so many lustres of years flourished under the influence of such pious doctrines, taught them in the excellent ministry of their late venerable pastor, whose gift and spirit, we hope, will long live and shine in this his grandson, to the end that they may abound yet more in all the lovely fruits of evangelical humility and thankfulness, to the glory of God.

To his blessing we commit them all, with this discourse, and every one that reads it; and are
Your servants in the gospel,
T. PRINCE.
W. COOPER.
Boston, August 17, 1731.

GOD GLORIFIED IN MAN'S DEPENDENCE[1]

A SERMON BY

JONATHAN EDWARDS, A.M.

That no flesh should glory in his presence. But of him are ye in Christ Jesus, who of God is made unto us wisdom, and righteousness, and sanctification, and redemption: that, according as it is written, He that glorieth, let him glory in the Lord.—1 CORINTHIANS 1:29, 30, 31.

Those Christians to whom the apostle directed this epistle, dwelt in a part of the world where human wisdom was in great repute; as the apostle observes in the 22nd verse of this chapter, "The Greeks seek after wisdom."

1 God Glorified in the Work of Redemption, by the Greatness of Man's Dependence upon Him, in the Whole of It. Preached on the Public Lecture in Boston, July 8, 1731; and published at the desire of several ministers and others in Boston who heard it.—This was the first piece published by Mr. Edwards.

Corinth was not far from Athens, that had been for many ages the most famous seat of philosophy and learning in the world. The apostle therefore observes to them, how God by the gospel destroyed, and brought to naught, their wisdom. The learned Grecians, and their great philosophers, by all their wisdom did not know God, they were not able to find out the truth in divine things. But, after they had done their utmost to no effect, it pleased God at length to reveal himself by the gospel, which they accounted foolishness. He "chose the foolish things of the world to confound the wise, and the weak things of the world to confound the things which are mighty, and the base things of the world, and things that are despised, yea, and things which are not, to bring to naught the things that are."[1] And the apostle informs them in the text why he thus did, *That no flesh should glory in his presence,* etc.—In which words may be observed,

1. What God aims at in the disposition of things in the affair of redemption, *viz.* that man should not glory in himself, but alone in God; *That no flesh should glory in his presence,— that, according as it is written, He that glorieth, let him glory in the Lord.*

2. How this end is attained in the work of redemption, *viz.* by that absolute and immediate dependence which men have upon God in that work, for all their good. Inasmuch as,

    First, All the good that they have is in and

1 1 Corinthians 1:27, 28.

through Christ; He *is made unto us wisdom, righteousness, sanctification, and redemption.* All the good of the fallen and redeemed creature is concerned in these four things, and cannot be better distributed than into them; but Christ is each of them to us, and we have none of them any otherwise than in him. *He is made of God unto us wisdom:* in him are all the proper good and true excellency of the understanding. Wisdom was a thing that the Greeks admired; but Christ is the true light of the world; it is through him alone that true wisdom is imparted to the mind. It is in and by Christ that we have *righteousness:* it is by being in him that we are justified, have our sins pardoned, and are received as righteous into God's favour. It is by Christ that we have *sanctification:* we have in him true excellency of heart as well as of understanding; and he is made unto us inherent as well as imputed righteousness. It is by Christ that we have *redemption*, or the actual deliverance from all misery, and the bestowment of all happiness and glory. Thus we have all our good by Christ, who is God.

Secondly, Another instance wherein our dependence on God for all our good appears, is this, That it is God that has given us Christ, that we might have these benefits through him; he *of God is made unto us wisdom, righteousness*, etc.

Thirdly, It is of him that we are in Christ Jesus, and come to have an interest in him, and so do receive those blessings which he is made unto us. It is God that gives us faith whereby we close with Christ.

So that in this verse is shown our dependence on each person in the Trinity for all our good. We are dependent on Christ the Son of God, as he is our wisdom, righteousness, sanctification, and redemption. We are dependent on the Father, who has given us Christ, and made him to be these things to us. We are dependent on the Holy Ghost, for it is *of him that we are in Christ Jesus;* it is the Spirit of God that gives faith in him, whereby we receive him, and close with him.

DOCTRINE

"God is glorified in the work of redemption in this, that there appears in it so absolute and universal a dependence of the redeemed on him."—Here I propose to show, 1*st*, that there is an absolute and universal dependence of the redeemed on God for all their good. And, 2*ndly*, That God hereby is exalted and glorified in the work of redemption.

I. There is an absolute and universal dependence of the redeemed on God. The nature and contrivance of our redemption is such, that the redeemed are in every thing directly, immediately, and entirely dependent on God: they are dependent on him for all, and are dependent on him every way.

The several ways wherein the dependence of one being may be upon another for its good, and wherein the redeemed of Jesus Christ depend on God for all their good, are these, *viz*. That they have all their good of him, and that they have all through him, and that they have all in him: That he is the *cause* and original whence all their good comes, therein it is *of* him; and that he is the *medium* by which it is obtained and conveyed, therein they have it *through* him; and that he is the *good itself* given and conveyed, therein it is *in* him. Now those that are redeemed by Jesus Christ do, in all these respects, very directly and entirely depend on God for their all.

First, The redeemed have all their good *of* God. God is the great *author* of it. He is the *first* cause of it; and not only so, but he is the *only* proper cause. It is of God that we have our Redeemer. It is God that has provided a Savior for us. Jesus Christ is not only of God in his person, as he is the only-begotten Son of God, but he is from God, as we are concerned in him, and in his office of Mediator. He is the gift of God to us: God chose and anointed him, appointed him his work, and sent him into the world. And as it is God that *gives*, so it is God that *accepts* the Saviour. He gives the purchaser, and he affords the thing purchased.

It is of God that Christ becomes ours, that we are brought to him, and are united to him. It is of God that we receive faith to close with him, that we may have an interest in him. Ephesians 2:8, "For by grace ye are saved, through faith;

and that not of yourselves, it is the gift of God."
It is of God that we actually receive all the benefits that Christ has purchased. It is God that
pardons and justifies, and delivers from going
down to hell; and into his favor the redeemed
are received, when they are justified. So it is God
that delivers from the dominion of sin, cleanses
us from our filthiness, and changes us from our
deformity. It is of God that the redeemed receive
all their true excellency, wisdom, and holiness;
and that two ways, *viz.* as the Holy Ghost by
whom these things are immediately wrought is
from God, proceeds from him, and is sent by him;
and also as the Holy Ghost himself is God, by
whose operation and indwelling the knowledge
of God and divine things, a holy disposition and
all grace, are conferred and upheld. And though
means are made use of in conferring grace on
men's souls, yet it is of God that we have these
means of grace, and it is he that makes them
effectual. It is of God that we have the Holy
Scriptures; they are his word. It is of God that
we have ordinances, and their efficacy depends
on the immediate influence of his Spirit. The
ministers of the gospel are sent of God, and all
their sufficiency is of him.—2 Corinthians 4:7,
"We have this treasure in earthen vessels, that
the excellency of the power may be of God, and
not of us." Their success depends entirely and
absolutely on the immediate blessing and influence of God.

    1. The redeemed have all from the *grace* of

God. It was of mere grace that God gave us his only-begotten Son. The grace is great in proportion to the excellency of what is given. The gift was infinitely precious, because it was of a person infinitely worthy, a person of infinite glory; and also because it was of a person infinitely near and dear to God. The grace is great in proportion to the benefit we have given us in him. The benefit is doubly infinite, in that in him we have deliverance from an infinite, because an eternal, misery, and do also receive eternal joy and glory. The grace in bestowing this gift is great in proportion to our unworthiness to whom it is given; instead of deserving such a gift, we merited infinitely ill of God's hands. The grace is great according to the manner of giving, or in proportion to the humiliation and expense of the method and means by which a way is made for our having the gift. He gave him to dwell amongst us; he gave him to us incarnate, or in our nature; and in the like though sinless infirmities. He gave him to us in a low and afflicted state; and not only so, but as slain, that he might be a feast for our souls.

The grace of God in bestowing this gift is most free. It was what God was under no obligation to bestow. He might have rejected fallen man, as he did the fallen angels. It was what we never did any thing to merit; it was given while we were yet enemies, and before we had so much as repented. It was from the love of God who saw no excellency in us to attract it;

and it was without expectation of ever being requited for it.—And it is from mere grace that the benefits of Christ are applied to such and such particular persons. Those that are called and sanctified are to attribute it alone to the good pleasure of God's goodness, by which they are distinguished. He is sovereign, and hath mercy on whom he will have mercy.

Man hath now a greater dependence on the grace of God than he had before the fall. He depends on the free goodness of God for much more than he did then. Then he depended on God's goodness for conferring the reward of perfect obedience; for God was not obliged to promise and bestow that reward. But now we are dependent on the grace of God for much more; we stand in need of grace, not only to bestow glory upon us, but to deliver us from hell and eternal wrath. Under the first covenant we depended on God's goodness to give us the reward of righteousness; and so we do now: but we stand in need of God's free and sovereign grace to give us that righteousness; to pardon our sin, and release us from the guilt and infinite demerit of it.

And as we are dependent on the goodness of God for more now than under the first covenant, so we are dependent on a much greater, more free and wonderful goodness. We are now more dependent on God's arbitrary and sovereign good pleasure. We were in our first estate dependent on God for holiness. We had our original righteousness from him; but then holiness was not bestowed in such a way of sovereign good pleasure as it is now. Man was created holy, for it became God to create holy all his reasonable creatures. It would have been a disparagement to the holiness of God's nature, if he had made an intelligent creature unholy. But now when fallen man is made holy, it is from mere and arbitrary grace; God may for ever deny holiness to the fallen creature if he pleases, without any disparagement to any of his perfections.

And we are not only indeed more dependent on the grace of God, but our dependence is much more conspicuous, because our own insufficiency and helplessness in ourselves is much more apparent in our fallen and undone state, than it was before we were either sinful or miserable. We are more apparently dependent on God for holiness, because we are first sinful, and utterly polluted, and afterward holy. So the production of the effect is sensible, and its derivation from God more obvious. If man was ever holy and always was so, it would not be so apparent, that he had not holiness necessarily, as an inseparable qualification of human nature. So we are more apparently dependent on free grace for the favour of God, for we are first justly the objects of his displeasure, and afterwards are received into favour. We are more apparently dependent on God for happiness, being first miserable, and afterwards happy. It is more apparently free and without merit in us, because we are actually without any kind of excellency to merit, if there could be any such thing as merit in creature-excellency. And we are not only without any true excellency, but are full of, and wholly defiled with, that which is infinitely odious. All our good is more apparently from God, because we are first naked and wholly without any good, and afterwards enriched with all good.

2. We receive all from the *power* of God. Man's redemption is often spoken of as a work of wonderful power as well as grace. The great power of God appears in bringing a sinner from his low state, from the depths of sin and misery, to such an exalted state of holiness and happiness. Ephesians 1:19. "And what is the exceeding greatness of his power to us-ward who believe, according to the working of his mighty power."—

We are dependent on God's power through every step of our redemption. We are dependent on the power of God to convert us, and give faith in Jesus Christ, and the new nature. It is a work of creation: "If any man be in Christ, he is a new creature," 2 Corinthians 5:17. "We are created in Christ Jesus," Ephesians 2:10. The fallen creature cannot attain to true holiness, but by being created again. Ephesians 4:24, "And that ye put on the new man, which after God is created in righteousness and true holiness." It is a raising from the dead. Colossians 2:12, 13. "Wherein also ye are risen with him through the faith of the operation of God, who hath raised him from the dead." Yea, it is a more glorious work of power than mere creation, or raising a dead body to life, in that the effect attained is greater and more excellent. That holy and happy being, and spiritual life, which is produced in the work of conversion, is a far greater and more glorious effect, than mere being and life. And the state from whence the change is made—a death in sin, a total corruption of nature, and depth of misery—is far more remote from the state attained, than mere death or non-entity.

It is by God's power also that we are preserved in a state of grace. 1 Peter 1:5. "Who are kept by the power of God through faith unto salvation." As grace is at first from God, so it is continually from him, and is maintained by him, as much as light in the atmosphere is all day long from the sun, as well as at first dawning, or sun-rising.—Men are dependent on the power of God for every exercise of grace, and for carrying on that work in the heart, for subduing sin and corruption, increasing holy principles, and enabling to bring forth fruit in good works. Man is dependent on divine power in bringing grace to its perfection, in making the soul completely amiable in Christ's glorious likeness, and filling of it with a satisfying joy and blessedness; and for the raising of the body to life, and to such a perfect state, that it shall be suitable for a habitation and organ for a soul so perfected and blessed. These are the most glorious effects of the power of God, that are seen in the series of God's acts with respect to the creatures.

Man was dependent on the power of God in his first estate, but he is more dependent on his power now; he needs God's power to do more things for him, and depends on a more wonderful exercise of his power. It was an effect of the power of God to make man holy at the first; but more remarkably so now, because there is a great deal of opposition and difficulty in the way. It is a more glorious effect of power to make that holy that was so depraved, and under the dominion of sin, than to confer holiness on that which before had nothing of the contrary. It is a more glorious work of power to rescue a soul out of the hands of the devil, and from the powers of darkness, and to bring it into a state of salvation, than to confer holiness where there was no prepossession or opposition. Luke 11:21, 22. "When a strong man armed keepeth his palace, his goods are in peace; but when a stronger than he shall come upon him, and overcome him, he taketh from him all his armour, wherein he trusted, and divideth his spoils." So it is a more glorious work of power to uphold a soul in a state of grace and holiness, and to carry it on till it is brought to glory, when there is so much sin remaining in the heart resisting, and Satan with all his might opposing, than it would have been to have kept man from falling at first, when Satan had nothing in man.—Thus we have shown how the redeemed are dependent on God for all their good, as they have all of him.

Secondly, They are also dependent on God for all, as they have all *through* him. God is the medium of it, as well as the author and fountain of it. All we have, wisdom, the pardon of sin, deliverance from hell, acceptance into God's favour, grace and holiness, true comfort and happiness, eternal life and glory, is from God by a Mediator; and this Mediator is God; which Mediator we have an absolute dependence upon, as he through whom we receive all. So that here is another way wherein we have our dependence on God for all good. God not only gives us the Mediator, and accepts his mediation, and of his power and grace bestows the things purchased by the Mediator; but he the Mediator is God.

Our blessings are what we have by purchase; and the purchase is made of God, the blessings are purchased of him, and God gives the purchaser; and not only so, but God is the purchaser. Yea God is both the purchaser and the price; for Christ, who is God, purchased these blessings for us, by offering up himself as the price of our salvation. He purchased eternal life by the sacrifice of himself. Hebrews 7:27. "He offered up himself." And 9:26. "He hath appeared to take away sin by the sacrifice of himself." Indeed it was the human nature that was offered; but it was the same person with the divine, and therefore was an infinite price.

As we thus have our good through God, we have a dependence on him in a respect that man in his first estate had not. Man was to have eternal life then through his own righteousness; so that he had partly a dependence upon what was in himself; for we have a dependence upon that through which we have our good, as well as that from which we have it; and though man's righteousness that he then depended on was indeed from God, yet it was his own, it was inherent in himself; so that his dependence was not so *immediately* on God. But now the righteousness that we are dependent on is not in ourselves, but in God. We are saved through the righteousness of Christ: He *is made unto us righteousness;* and therefore is prophesied of, Jeremiah 23:6, under that name, "the Lord our righteousness." In that the righteousness we are justified by is the righteousness of Christ, it is the righteousness of God. 2 Corinthians 5:21. "That we might be made the righteousness of God in him."—Thus in redemption we have not only all things of God, but by and through him, 1 Corinthians 8:6. "But to us there is but one God, the Father, of whom are all things, and we in him; and one Lord Jesus Christ, by whom are all things, and we by him."

Thirdly, The redeemed have all their good *in God*. We not only have it of him, and through him, but it consists in him; he is all our good.— The good of the redeemed is either objective or inherent. By their objective good, I mean that extrinsic object, in the possession and enjoyment of which they are happy. Their inherent good is that excellency or pleasure which is in the soul itself. With respect to both of which the redeemed have all their good in God, or which is the same thing, God himself is all their good.

1. The redeemed have all their *objective* good in God. God himself is the great good which they are brought to the possession and enjoyment of by redemption. He is the highest good, and the sum of all that good which Christ purchased. God is the inheritance of the saints; he is the portion of their souls. God is their wealth and treasure, their food, their life, their dwelling-place, their ornament and diadem, and their everlasting honour and glory. They have none in heaven but God; he is the great good which the redeemed are received to at death, and which they are to rise to at the end of the world. The Lord God is the light of the heavenly Jerusalem; and is the "river of the water of life" that runs, and "the tree of life that grows, in the midst of the paradise of God." The glorious excellencies and beauty of God will be what will forever entertain the minds of the saints, and the love of God will be their everlasting feast. The redeemed will indeed enjoy other things; they will enjoy the angels, and will enjoy one another: but that which they shall enjoy in the angels, or each other, or in any thing else whatsoever that will yield them delight and happiness, will be what shall be seen of God in them.

2. The redeemed have all their *inherent* good in God. Inherent good is twofold; it is either

excellency or pleasure. These the redeemed not only derive from God, as caused by him, but have them in him. They have spiritual excellency and joy by a kind of participation of God. They are made excellent by a communication of God's excellency. God puts his own beauty, *i.e.* his beautiful likeness, upon their souls. They are made partakers of the divine nature, or moral image of God, 2 Peter 1:4. They are holy by being made partakers of God's holiness, Hebrews 12:10. The saints are beautiful and blessed by a communication of God's holiness and joy, as the moon and planets are bright by the sun's light. The saint hath spiritual joy and pleasure by a kind of effusion of God on the soul. In these things the redeemed have communion with God; that is, they partake with him and of him.

The saints have both their spiritual excellency and blessedness by the gift of the Holy Ghost, and his dwelling in them. They are not only caused by the Holy Ghost, but are in him as their principle. The Holy Spirit becoming an inhabitant, is a vital principle in the soul. He, acting in, upon, and with the soul, becomes a fountain of true holiness and joy, as a spring is of water, by the exertion and diffusion of itself. John 4:14. "But whosoever drinketh of the water that I shall give him, shall never thirst; but the water that I shall give him, shall be in him a well of water springing up into everlasting life." Compared with chapter 7:38, 39. "He that believeth on me, as the Scripture hath said, out of his belly shall flow rivers of living water; but this spake he of the Spirit, which they that believe on him should receive." The sum of what Christ has purchased for us, is that spring of water spoken of in the former of those places, and those rivers of living water spoken of in the latter. And the sum of the blessings, which the redeemed shall receive in heaven, is that river of water of life that proceeds from the throne of God and the Lamb, Revelation 22:1. Which doubtless signifies the same with those rivers of living water, explained, John 7:38, 39; which is elsewhere called the "river of God's pleasures." Herein consists the fullness of good, which the saints receive of Christ. It is by partaking of the Holy Spirit, that they have communion with Christ in his fullness. God hath given the Spirit, not by measure unto him; and they do receive of his fullness, and grace for grace. This is the sum of the saints' inheritance; and therefore that little of the Holy Ghost which believers have in this world, is said to be the earnest of their inheritance, 2 Corinthians 1:22. "Who hath also sealed us, and given us the earnest of the Spirit in our hearts." And chapter 5:5, "Now he that hath wrought us for the self-same thing, is God, who also hath given unto us the earnest of the Spirit." And Ephesians 1:13, 14, "Ye were sealed with that holy Spirit of promise, which is the earnest of our inheritance, until the redemption of the purchased possession."

The Holy Spirit and good things are spoken

of in Scripture as the same; as if the Spirit of God communicated to the soul, comprised all good things, Matthew 7:11. "How much more shall your heavenly Father give good things to them that ask him?" In Luke it is, chapter 11:13, "How much more shall your heavenly Father give the Holy Spirit to them that ask him?" This is the sum of the blessings that Christ died to procure, and the subject of gospel-promises. Galatians 3:13–14, "He was made a curse for us, that we might receive the promise of the Spirit through faith." The Spirit of God is the great promise of the Father, Luke 24:49. "Behold, I send the promise of my Father upon you." The Spirit of God therefore is called "the Spirit of promise," Ephesians 1:13. This promised thing Christ received, and had given into his hand, as soon as he had finished the work of our redemption, to bestow on all that he had redeemed; Acts 2:33. "Therefore being by the right hand of God exalted, and having received of the Father the promise of the Holy Ghost, he hath shed forth this, which ye both see and hear." So that all the holiness and happiness of the redeemed is in God. It is in the communications, indwelling, and acting of the Spirit of God. Holiness and happiness is in the fruit, here and hereafter, because God dwells in them, and they in God.

Thus God has given us the Redeemer, and it is by him that our good is purchased. So God is the Redeemer and the price; and he also is the good purchased. So that all that we have is of God, and through him, and in him. Romans 11:36. "For of him, and through him, and to him, or in him, are all things." The same in the Greek that is here rendered *to him*, is rendered *in him*, 1 Corinthians 8:6.

II. God is glorified in the work of redemption by this means, *viz.* By there being so great and universal a dependence of the redeemed on him.

1. Man hath so much the greater occasion and obligation to notice and acknowledge God's perfections and all-sufficiency. The greater the creature's dependence is on God's perfections, and the greater concern he has with them, so much the greater occasion has he to take notice of them. So much the greater concern any one has with and dependence upon the power and grace of God, so much the greater occasion has he to take notice of that power and grace. So much the greater and more immediate dependence there is on the divine holiness, so much the greater occasion to take notice of and acknowledge that. So much the greater and more absolute dependence we have on the divine perfections, as belonging to the several persons of the Trinity, so much the greater occasion have we to observe and own the divine glory of each of them. That which we are most concerned with, is surely most in the way of our observation and notice; and this kind of concern with any thing, *viz.* dependence, does especially tend to command and oblige the attention and observation. Those things that we are not much dependent

upon, it is easy to neglect; but we can scarce do any other than mind that which we have a great dependence on. By reason of our so great dependence on God, and his perfections, and in so many respects, he and his glory are the more directly set in our view, which way soever we turn our eyes.

We have the greater occasion to take notice of God's all-sufficiency, when all our sufficiency is thus every way of him. We have the more occasion to contemplate him as an infinite good, and as the fountain of all good. Such a dependence on God demonstrates his all-sufficiency. So much as the dependence of the creature is on God, so much the greater does the creature's emptiness in himself appear; and so much the greater the creature's emptiness, so much the greater must the fullness of the Being be who supplies him. Our having all *of* God, shows the fullness of his power and grace; our having all *through* him, shows the fullness of his merit and worthiness; and our having all *in* him, demonstrates his fullness of beauty, love, and happiness. And the redeemed, by reason of the greatness of their dependence on God, have not only so much the greater occasion, but obligation to contemplate and acknowledge the glory and fullness of God. How unreasonable and ungrateful should we be, if we did not acknowledge that sufficiency and glory which we absolutely, immediately, and universally depend upon!

2. Hereby is demonstrated how great God's

glory is considered comparatively, or as compared with the creature's.—By the creature being thus wholly and universally dependent on God, it appears that the creature is nothing, and that God is all. Hereby it appears that God is infinitely above us; that God's strength, and wisdom, and holiness, are infinitely greater than ours. However great and glorious the creature apprehends God to be, yet if he be not sensible of the difference between God and him, so as to see that God's glory is great, compared with his own, he will not be disposed to give God the glory due to his name. If the creature in any respects sets himself upon a level with God, or exalts himself to any competition with him, however he may apprehend that great honour and profound respect may belong to God from those that are at a greater distance, he will not be so sensible of its being due from him. So much the more men exalt themselves, so much the less will they surely be disposed to exalt God. It is certainly what God aims at in the disposition of things in redemption, (if we allow the Scriptures to be a revelation of God's mind,) that God should appear full, and man in himself empty, that God should appear all, and man nothing. It is God's declared design that others should not "glory in his presence;" which implies that it is his design to advance his own comparative glory. So much the more man "glories in God's presence," so much the less glory is ascribed to God.

3. By its being thus ordered, that the

creature should have so absolute and universal a dependence on God, provision is made that God should have our whole souls, and should be the object of our undivided respect. If we had our dependence partly on God, and partly on something else, man's respect would be divided to those different things on which he had dependence. Thus it would be if we depended on God only for a part of our good, and on ourselves, or some other being, for another part: or if we had our good only from God, and through another that was not God, and in something else distinct from both, our hearts would be divided between the good itself, and him from whom, and him through whom, we received it. But now there is no occasion for this, God being not only he from or of whom we have all good, but also through whom, and is that good itself, that we have from him and through him. So that whatsoever there is to attract our respect, the tendency is still directly towards God, all unites in him as the centre.

USE

1. We may here observe the marvelous wisdom of God, in the work of redemption. God hath made man's emptiness and misery, his low, lost, and ruined state, into which he sunk by the fall, an occasion of the greater advancement of his own glory, as in other ways, so particularly in this, that there is now much more universal and apparent dependence of man on God. Though

God be pleased to lift man out of that dismal abyss of sin and woe into which he was fallen, and exceedingly to exalt him in excellency and honour, and to a high pitch of glory and blessedness, yet the creature hath nothing in any respect to glory of; all the glory evidently belongs to God, all is in a mere, and most absolute, and divine dependence on the Father, Son, and Holy Ghost. And each person of the Trinity is equally glorified in this work: there is an absolute dependence of the creature on every one for all: all is of the Father, all through the Son, and all in the Holy Ghost. Thus God appears in the work of redemption as all in all. It is fit that he who is, and there is none else, should be the Alpha and Omega, the first and the last, the all and the only, in this work.

2. Hence those doctrines and schemes of divinity that are in any respect opposite to such an absolute and universal dependence on God, derogate from his glory, and thwart the design of our redemption. And such are those schemes that put the creature in God's stead, in any of the mentioned respects, that exalt man into the place of either Father, Son, or Holy Ghost, in any thing pertaining to our redemption. However they may allow of a dependence of the redeemed on God, yet they deny a dependence that is so *absolute* and universal. They own an entire dependence on God for *some* things, but not for others; they own that we depend on God for the gift and acceptance of a Redeemer, but

deny so absolute a dependence on him for the obtaining of an *interest* in the Redeemer. They own an absolute dependence on the Father for giving his Son, and on the Son for working out redemption, but not so entire a dependence on the Holy Ghost for *conversion*, and a being in Christ, and so coming to a title to his benefits. They own a dependence on God for *means* of grace, but not absolutely for the benefit and success of those means; a partial dependence on the power of God, for obtaining and exercising holiness, but not a mere dependence on the arbitrary and sovereign grace of God. They own a dependence on the free grace of God for a reception into his favour, so far that it is without any proper merit, but not as it is without being attracted, or moved with any excellency. They own a partial dependence on Christ, as he through whom we have life, as having purchased new terms of life, but still hold that the righteousness through which we have life is inherent in ourselves, as it was under the first covenant. Now whatever scheme is inconsistent with our *entire* dependence on God for all, and of having all of him, through him, and in him, it is repugnant to the design and tenor of the gospel, and robs it of that which God accounts its lustre and glory.

3. Hence we may learn a reason why faith is that by which we come to have an interest in this redemption; for there is included in the nature of faith, a sensible acknowledgment of

absolute dependence on God in this affair. It is
very fit that it should be required of all, in order
to their having the benefit of this redemption,
that they should be sensible of, and acknowledge, their dependence on God for it. It is by this
means that God hath contrived to glorify himself in redemption; and it is fit that he should at
least have this glory of those that are the sub-
jects of this redemption, and have the benefit of
it.—Faith is a sensibleness of what is real in the
work of redemption; and the soul that believes
doth entirely depend on God for all salvation, in
its own sense and act. Faith abases men, and
exalts God; it gives all the glory of redemption
to him alone. It is necessary in order to saving
faith, that man should be emptied of himself,
be sensible that he is "wretched, and miserable,
and poor, and blind, and naked." Humility is
a great ingredient of true faith: he that truly
receives redemption, receives it as a little child,
Mark 10:15. "Whosoever shall not receive the
kingdom of heaven as a little child, he shall not
enter therein." It is the delight of a believing
soul to abase itself and exalt God alone: that is
the language of it, Psalm 115:1. "Not unto us, O
Lord, not unto us, but to thy name give glory."

4. Let us be exhorted to exalt God alone, and
ascribe to him all the glory of redemption. Let
us endeavour to obtain, and increase in, a sensibleness of our great dependence on God, to have
our eye to him alone, to mortify a self-dependent
and self-righteous disposition. Man is naturally

exceeding prone to exalt himself, and depend on his own power or goodness; as though from himself he must expect happiness. He is prone to have respect to enjoyments alien from God and his Spirit, as those in which happiness is to be found.—But this doctrine should teach us to exalt God *alone;* as by trust and reliance, so by praise. *Let him that glorieth, glory in the Lord.* Hath any man hope that he is converted, and sanctified, and that his mind is endowed with true excellency and spiritual beauty? that his sins are forgiven, and he received into God's favour, and exalted to the honour and blessedness of being his child, and an heir of eternal life? let him give God all the glory; who alone makes him to differ from the worst of men in this world, or the most miserable of the damned in hell. Hath any man much comfort and strong hope of eternal life, let not his hope lift him up, but dispose him the more to abase himself, to reflect on his own exceeding unworthiness of such a favour, and to exalt God alone. Is any man eminent in holiness, and abundant in good works, let him take nothing of the glory of it to himself, but ascribe it to him whose "workmanship we are, created in Christ Jesus unto good works."

NOTES

NOTES

NOTES

MAN'S QUESTIONS & GOD'S ANSWERS

Am I accountable to God?
"Every one of us shall give account of himself to God." (Romans 14:12).

Has God seen all my ways?
"All things are naked and opened unto the eyes of Him with whom we have to do." (Hebrews 4:13).

Does He charge me with sin?
"The Scripture hath concluded all under sin." (Galatians 3:22).
"All have sinned." (Romans 3:23).

Will He punish sin?
"The soul that sinneth, it shall die." (Ezekiel 18:4).
"For the wages of sin is death." (Romans 6:23).

Must I perish?
"God is not willing that any perish, but that all should come to repentance." (2 Peter 3:9).

How can I escape?
"Believe on the Lord Jesus Christ, and thou shalt be saved." (Acts 16:31).

Is He able to save me?
"He is able also to save them to the uttermost that come unto God by Him." (Hebrews 7:25).

Is He willing?
"Christ Jesus came into the world to save sinners." (1 Timothy 1:15).

Am I saved on believing?
"He that believeth on the Son hath everlasting life." (John 3:36).

Can I be saved now?
"Now is the accepted time; behold, now is the day of salvation." (2 Corinthians 6:2).

As I am?
"Him that cometh to Me I will in no wise cast out." (John 6:37).

Shall I not fall away?
"Him that is able to keep you from falling." (Jude 24).

If saved, how should I live?
"They which live should not henceforth live unto themselves, but unto Him which died for them." (2 Corinthians 5:15).

What about death, and eternity?
"I go to prepare a place for you; that where I am, there ye may be also." (John 14:2, 3).

www.ingramcontent.com/pod-product-compliance
Lightning Source LLC
Chambersburg PA
CBHW020444030426
42337CB00014B/1384